HOPE

Encouraging Stories and Biblical Promises

John G. Gage

"And you will feel secure, because there is hope..." .(Job 11:18)

TABLE OF CONTENTS

HOPE

Encouraging Stories and Bible Promises

John G Gage

"Joseph, a Levite and a Cypriot by birth, the one the apostles called Barnabas, which is translated 'Son of Encouragement,' sold a field he owned, brought the money, and laid it at the apostles' feet." (Acts 4:36-37)

Every time we see Barnabas, he is encouraging someone. His name appears 23 times in the book of Acts alone!

In Acts 4 he encourages the church by financially supporting their ministry.

In Acts 9 he introduces Saul to the apostles at Jerusalem, validates his testimony and authenticates his ministry, and the skeptical apostles finally accept him as Paul.

In Acts 11 he is sent by the church at Jerusalem to minister to the Gentiles in Antioch where he encourages the Jewish community to accept the Gentile believers.

In Acts 15 Paul and John Mark have a disagreement and Paul refuses to include John Mark on future missionary journeys, so Barnabas takes John Mark, Paul takes Silas and both teams have effective ministry from that point on.

Everyone needs an encourager. The word "encourage" means "to instill courage". Everyone at some point gets weak, faint and afraid, and needs someone to come alongside, lift them up and give them the courage to continue the journey.

Derek Redmond was a British runner. In 1985 he broke the British record for the 400- meter race. In 1986 he was on the 4 x 400 team that won gold at the European Championships. In 1987 he competed on the 4 x 400 team that won silver at the World Championships. He had prepared hard for the Seoul Olympics but pulled out of the final race with a torn Achilles tendon. He struggled with injury throughout his career, having 8 surgeries by the 1992 Olympics in Barcelona.

At Barcelona he was favored to win the 400- meter race. He won the first two heats easily. In the semi-final he started strong, and at about the half -way point he heard a loud "snap" and fell to the track in pain with a torn hamstring muscle. His dad, Jim Redmond, pushed his way past security and onto the track, rushed to his son's side, lifted Derek to his feet, and supporting his son, they completed the final lap together to the standing ovation of 65,000 Olympic fans.

Be an encourager. Help someone finish well. We all need a Jim Redmond in our lives to help support us and to help us complete the journey.

2- BALANCE FOR THE WIN

I have a replica of the 1999 Tony Stewart car which is very special. WHY? Because in 1999, Tony ran the Indy 500 in an open wheel Indy car and finished ninth. Then he flew to Charlotte, NC and ran the Coca Cola 600 in a Nascar machine and finished fourth. Two top 10 finishes on the same day in two of the most prestigious automobile races in the world.

Why does someone push himself so hard? It could be for recognition, or to impress someone. It could be to please a spouse or car owner, or because of the payday. Perhaps it is to prove to oneself that they can accomplish the unthinkable.

I have known pastors who were tireless in ministry. One friend pushed himself so hard that he ended up in a mental hospital. It is admirable to give your best, but it is foolish to fail to work a balanced life. The apostle Paul put it this way:

"Pay careful attention then, to how you walk-not as unwise people but as wise- Making the most of the time, because the days are evil. So don't be foolish but understand what the will of the Lord is." (Eph. 5:15 HCSB)

I have two pastor friends who exemplify this advice. Both were athletes and both work out physically every day. Both balance family time with work time, and both have accomplished the unimaginable because they have learned how to manage their time to make the most of work time so they can invest family time without feeling guilty that work was left unfinished. They have learned the blessing of balance.

Prioritize, give your best effort, surround yourself with others who can help you accomplish your goals. But balance work and play, family and personal study. I once heard an evangelist say, "I would rather burn out than rust out." A person who lives a balanced life should do neither. One can race 1100 miles if their mind and body are fresh and prepared. That is accomplished by practicing balance.

Ted had just finished pharmacy school and wanted to open a drug store. Together with his wife Dorothy they looked for a location that would have both a good church and a drug store for sale, and they found just the right combination in a little town that Ted's father-in -law called "God-forsaken". They created a makeshift home by hanging a blanket in the back of the store and began work. But business was bad...really bad. It was the middle of the Great Depression and day after day they struggled to make ends meet. One day Dorothy retired to the back of the store to take a nap, but soon returned to where Ted was swatting flies with a rolled -up newspaper.

"Too hot to sleep?" Ted inquired.

"No, I can't sleep for all the cars passing by on route 16A! It is just too noisy!"

Suddenly Dorothy's countenance brightened. "Do you know what those cars need? WATER! Every one of the people in those cars are hot and thirsty! Let's advertise free ice water and maybe they will stop in!"

And Ted, with the help of a high school boy, made some makeshift signs and placed them along the highway advertising free ice water. Soon cars were stopping to take advantage of the offer and began buying ice cream and other treats to be refreshed on their journey. And the store grew. The next summer they hired eight girls to help, and today they have over 2 million visitors a year in the tiny town of Wall, South Dakota, where Wall Drug has become a popular tourist destination...and they still offer free ice water!

Do you ever feel like your situation is hopeless? That no matter how hard you try, you seem to fail over and over again? Be patient. Be creative. Find a need and meet it. Trust God and work hard. Those two things go hand in hand. The Apostle Paul told the church at Thessalonica, "We worked night and day, laboring and toiling so that we would not be a burden to any of you." (2 Thess. 3:8) And don't give up! Every lasting work has two parts: Our part and God's part. Do your part to the best of your ability, and trust God to do His part. Someone needs the ice water that only you can provide.

4-MOVING FORWARD

Billy Mills was a Lakota Indian from Pine Ridge, South Dakota. At the age of eight he lost his mother to an illness, and four years later his father passed away. He learned both boxing and running, and eventually focused on the 10,000-meter race. Mills was a type 2 diabetic and was constantly concerned that long distance running would upset his blood sugar, but he continued running anyway. At the 1964 Olympics he qualified at a time that was a full minute behind his closest competitor, but at the event he kept pace with the other three front runners. On the final lap he was pushed by two other runners but recovered and sprinted to victory...a win that is still considered the greatest upset in Olympic history. Incredibly, Mills never owned a new pair of shoes until the night before the Olympic games.

We tend to give up too quickly. When things get tough, the temptation is to bail, rather than to keep moving forward. The Apostle Paul refers to this tendency in Philippians 3:13:

Brothers, I do not consider myself to have taken hold of it.

*But **one** thing I do: Forgetting what is behind and **reaching forward** to what is ahead,*

I pursue as my goal the prize promised by God's heavenly call in Christ Jesus.

Let me challenge you to always look forward. Forget the failures of the past. They just serve as teaching tools to help us avoid future mistakes. When I was learning how to ride a motorcycle, I asked a veteran rider how to correctly operate the clutch. His answer was a deep insight,

"Whatever it takes to keep moving forward!"

I have applied that wisdom often in my life. Forgetting what is behind, *press on* toward what is ahead. Learn from the past but don't dwell there. One can't make progress if their focus is constantly on the rear -view mirror.

5-DWELLING

We have just enjoyed a week with my son, his wife and four precious daughters who have been visiting from California. While the two older girls were at our church camp and the eight-year- old visited with friends, I had a unique opportunity to bond with Cate, the two year old. She would crawl up in my lap and request, "Can we watch Paw Patrol??" or "Can I play on your phone?" (How can a two-year old manipulate my phone better than I can???)

Sometimes her request would be, "Can I have cereal Life?" Which being interpreted is, "May I have some Life cereal?" How precious to sit on the couch together, her hand in mine, and just enjoy being together!

Psalm 27 was written when David was in a difficult place. In his trial he found peace dwelling in the presence of Jehovah. Verse 4 expresses his faith in his Heavenly Father, "I have asked one thing of the Lord; it is what I desire: to dwell in the house of the Lord all the days of my life, gazing on the beauty of the Lord and seeking him in His temple." The word "dwell" carries the thought of shelter, of protection in His presence. No matter how tall the waves or rough the wind, there is a sense of calm peace and protection "Under the shelter of Your (His) Wings." (Ps. 61:4)

God designed us for relationship. That requires both presence and communication. And that requires time. How precious it is to get off the computer, put the phone down, turn the tv off, and just enjoy fellowship with the heavenly Father. How much we forfeit when we fail to spend time enjoying His presence. When we are in the midst of the storm, only His presence can create a calm, confident heart.

David ends this Psalm with a sense of confidence:

"Wait for the Lord; Be strong and courageous. Wait for the Lord." *(V. 14)*

There is confidence and peace in His presence, but to appropriate the blessings one must invest in the relationship. "You cheer him with joy in Your presence." (Ps. 21:6)

In 1970 the Sound Generation was invited to perform at the half time of a New York Jets-New Orleans Saints pre-season game at the old Tulane stadium in New Orleans. Several things about this performance stand out in my memory.

As I stepped to the mic to play the opening trumpet fanfare to God Bless America, the stadium lights were dimmed, and 80,000 fans lit matches and lighters. The memory of the glow of Patriotism in the stadium that night still gives me goosebumps. After the game we were invited to a party celebrating the players. I was 5'6", and the shortest pro football player in that room was a full foot taller than I was. Talk about intimidated! I hid in a corner eating my cookie and trying to be invisible. But even though these players were giants, there was an eerie silence in the room that night. This was the game before the final cut that would give each team the maximum number of players allowed on their rosters, and no one felt secure. There was a sense of...*fear* in the room. I don't attend a lot of parties, but that was the quietest one I had ever observed!!

Do you ever feel like you are in a room full of giants? Are circumstances threatening? Are your challenges larger than you can handle? Are relationships disappointing and challenging? Are finances a burden that threaten to drown you? Listen to the words of the Biblical character David when he faced a threatening giant:

"Then all the world will know that Israel has a God, and this whole assembly will know that it is not by sword or by spear that

the Lord saves, for the battle is the Lord's. He will hand you over to us." (1 Samuel 17:47

If you don't think you can handle your giants, you are correct. But there is Someone who can. Trust Him. Completely. Be patient. Remember the words of the prophet Zechariah, "Not by strength or by might, but by *My Spirit*, says the Lord of Hosts." (Zech. 4:6)

The name "Lord of Hosts" indicates the highest level of military authority. It is like saying "Four-star General" or "Admiral." In the words of the hymn by Charles Albert Tindley, "Take your burden to the Lord and leave it there."

7-MANNA

Exodus 16 tells the story of God's provision for the physical needs of the Children of Israel as they left Egypt and headed toward the land God had promised them. There are a few interesting facts about manna from which we can draw some conclusions:

- Manna means "What is it," because when it appeared, the Children of Israel had seen nothing like it before.
- They were to gather just what they needed six days each week (About 2 quarts per day). If they gathered more than was necessary, the remainder would be filled with worms the next day and would stink. If they gathered less than they needed, it would miraculously be enough until the following day.
- According to the Believer's Bible Commentary, manna was a small, round, white wafer and tasted like honey. (Even the

Israelites liked biscuits with honey!!) It could be baked, boiled or eaten raw.

- On the sixth day they were to gather enough for two days, because no manna fell on the Sabbath, which was to be a day of rest. This is the first mention of a "sabbath" in the Bible, well before the ten commandments were given.
- Manna fell six days a week for forty years, ceasing when the Children of Israel entered the promised land.

There is one primary lesson (among many others) that we can glean from this passage. The Israelites were to gather only what they needed. If they gathered more, the surplus would spoil. If they gathered less, they would still have enough. The median world-wide income is $2,800 per year. The average American earns $70,784 per year. That means that the average American earns 25 times more than the average median income for people around the world. Therefore, the average American has "extra" beyond what they need to support their families. We each have a choice to make. We can either spend the extra or store it in stuff that fills our garages and attics or invest it in ministry where God will multiply it and use it for His glory.

I believe the Lord's return is imminent. We must "redeem the time" while we can and invest in Kingdom work while there is still time. Find a ministry that you can support and invest your extra wisely.

Put your financial blessings to work for Kingdom growth. This investment will pay big dividends.

8-THE ART OF COMPLAINING

Here are a few interesting excerpts from the Old Testament:

"Then Moses told Aaron, "Say to the entire Israelite community, 'Come before the Lord, for He has heard your complaints.'" (Ex. 16:9)

"So the people complained to Moses, "Give us water to drink." (Ex. 17:2)

"Now the people began complaining openly before the Lord about hardship." (Numbers 11:1)

'ALL the Israelites complained about Moses and Aaron…" (Numbers 14:2)

The Cambridge dictionary defines *complain* as "to say that something is wrong or not satisfactory." In Exodus 17 the word translated "complain" means "to quarrel or argue." In Numbers 11 the word means "to wrestle" or "to wrangle." The Israelites have been rescued from horrible, devastating work conditions as slaves in Egypt, and God is teaching them to trust Him for their every need. The desert is a harsh place. For Israel it was a training camp, preparing them for what they would face in the future. But rather than being grateful for their miraculous escape from bondage, they argued, wrestled with their leadership, complained that they would have been better off back in Egypt and they failed to remember the miracles God had accomplished to bring them to this place.

In Exodus 16 God hears their complaint and meets their need with quail and manna.

In Exodus 17 God patiently listens to their grumbling and provides water.

By Numbers 11 they are tired of the manna God has been providing, and they tell Moses, "We remember the free fish we ate in Egypt, along with the cucumbers, melons, leeks, onions and garlic. But now our appetites are gone; there's nothing to look at but this manna!"

And God gets angry. After all He has done for them, all they can see is inconvenience and lack of variety in their diet. Their needs have all been met, but they want more...so much more that they begin to yearn for the food that was identified with their bondage!

"Grumbling complaints...declare that God is not sufficiently good, faithful, loving, wise, powerful or competent." (Jon Bloom, desiringgod.org) Be very careful about complaining. God may be trying to accomplish something in you that can only come through difficulty and challenges. Remember His faithfulness in the past and be grateful. Be patient as He works in and through you to accomplish His will. Complaining just expresses dissatisfaction at the way God is handling things.

9-EILEEN

"The diligent hand will rule, but laziness will lead to forced labor". (Prov. 12:24)

Eileen grew up in upstate New York. Her family didn't have much, so she put herself through community college by working several part time jobs. She went on to earn a bachelor's degree in mathematics and economics from Syracuse University, then a master's in operations research from Stanford and a master's in Space Systems Management from Webster University. In 1986 she accepted a position at the Air Force Academy teaching math, but also realized a life-long dream of flying by becoming a test pilot at Edwards Air Force Base, flying some 26 types of aircraft in a single year. In 1995 Eileen Collins became the first woman to pilot a space shuttle, flying the shuttle *Discovery* to the Mir space station.

I have no sympathy for those who complain that they never get a break. "Life is so tough! I just can't get ahead!" Yes, life can be difficult. But everyone has opportunity if they will look beyond their perceived limitations, be creative and seek to discover ways to improve their circumstances.

- Albert Einstein didn't speak until he was three years old and was considered lazy and dumb by his schoolteachers…but he discovered the theory of relativity.
- Vincent Van Gogh created over 900 paintings but only sold *one* during his lifetime.
- Thomas Edison failed almost 10,000 times before he finally invented the light bulb.
- Benjamin Franklin's parents couldn't afford to educate him, so through reading he educated himself, becoming a great inventor and politician.

In 1 Thess. 3:10, Paul admonishes the church in Thessalonica,

"If anyone isn't willing to work, he should not eat." (HCSB)

The writer of the book of Proverbs puts it this way,

"The diligent hand will rule, but laziness will lead to forced labor". *(Prov. 12:24)*

Don't give up. Don't expect someone else to provide for you. Continue to explore options and seek answers until a path becomes clear to you. You can do it, if you will just be diligent.

10-TREASURE OR TURDS?

I was around seven years old while playing one day under our pine tree. Suddenly I saw what appeared to be a bunch of marbles half hidden under a branch! I excitedly gathered them up, put them in my hat and ran to show Mom my new-found treasure.

"Silly boy" She responded. "Those are rabbit turds! Put them back where you found them!"

So, I dutifully placed them back where I had found them...under the pine tree where they belonged.

How often have we mistaken rabbit turds for treasure! It may be that relationship that seems so desirable, but the end result is disastrous. Perhaps we have spent a good portion of our lives pursuing fame or financial gain, only to discover that we would have been much better off to have spent our time searching the treasures of God's Word or investing in our family.

Isaiah 44:9 says, "All who make idols are nothing, and the things they treasure are worthless." How foolish to spend a lifetime pursuing worthless treasures. Be very careful to differentiate between treasure and worthless junk. Invest in those actions and activities that will pay the highest dividend, and when you look back over a lifetime of investing, you won't be left holding a hatful of rabbit turds.

11-TRUE TREASURE

"For where your treasure is, there your heart will be also."
(Matthew 6:21)

Sometimes what appears to have great value is actually worthless. Perhaps you can recall a time when you were fooled into believing that something very temporary would last forever. Perhaps this was true of a friendship!

We all need to be incredibly careful with relationships. God designed us for fellowship and mutual encouragement, but if we allow the flesh to control our feelings for one another, we can end up in a world of hurt. Here is one scenario:

Susie came to her worship leader James for counsel. Her marriage wasn't as fulfilling as it once was, and her husband seemed inattentive. James listened, and offered some wisdom, but deep down he wanted to rescue her, to be her knight in shining armor who would offer her the love she deserved and needed…but he kept those thoughts to himself.

The next day Susie called James to thank him for meeting with her. She had some more questions but suggested that they meet at a nearby Starbucks to avoid being seen together at church two days in a row. James agreed, and they met. Now James began to confide in Susie some of the challenges with his own marriage…how his wife's job and care of the kids left her so tired that she had no strength left to invest in their relationship, and they seemed increasingly like two strangers living in the same house.

Over the next several months James and Susie met more often, sharing with each other. One day they met at Starbucks and after their meeting James walked Susie to her car at the back of the parking lot. He slipped in the passenger side while she got behind the wheel. As they chatted, James reached over and pulled Susie's face toward his. It seemed very natural to exchange a kiss. As James pulled her head toward his, his hand brushed against her breast, and she didn't resist. He positioned his body to accommodate her outstretched hand, and at that moment they both made a fateful decision. They decided that a fleeting, transient moment of passion was more important than the vows they had each made to their respective spouses. It was more important than the commitment they had to their church or their pastor. It overshadowed the example they wanted to be for their children, their colleagues, their friends. It became more important than their relationship to Jesus.

"But Jesus wants me to be happy!"

No, Jesus wants you to be obedient. Obedience always precedes happiness.

"But my heart feels so complete, so content with her!"

"The heart is more deceitful than anything else, and incurable- who can understand it?" (Jer. 17:9)

Sexual sin is addictive. It always yearns for more. Soon James and Susie were seeking places to be alone...her house, his house, the church basement, a motel room.

Eventually the guilt became overwhelming to Susie, and she confessed everything to her husband. His first phone call was to their pastor. The next call was to James' wife. Both families were irreparably fractured. Their children felt betrayed and confused. Both reputations were damaged beyond repair. And James lost his ministry.

John 8:44 says, *"The Devil...is a liar and the father of liars". I Peter 5:8 warns, "Be serious! Be alert! Your adversary the Devil is prowling around like a roaring lion, looking for anyone he can devour."*

Make the decision early on in ministry that you will finish well. Place safeguards around your relationships to protect you from any possibility of moral failure. *"Guard your heart above all else, for it is the source of life." (Proverbs 4:23)*

"...Where your treasure is, there your heart will be also." Treasure your spouse, your family, your ministry. Hide God's Word in your heart. Make a commitment early on to honor your marriage vows no matter what. Make a commitment to finish well, and God will provide the strength and the courage to do what it takes to honor your commitments. Yearn for the day you will hear your Savior say, "Well done, good and faithful servant!" And you will realize that the things you think you may have sacrificed along the way really weren't treasures at all.

12-A DIFFERENT GIFT

For several years I was the conductor of a 118- piece string orchestra at Stockdale High School, Bakersfield, California. It was a wonderful experience, and I wouldn't trade those days for anything in the world. When you have that many students in one ensemble, you discover that for some of them, playing the violin isn't their primary gift!

Each year we created a logo for an orchestra t-shirt. We always allowed students to submit design ideas, then the group would vote for their favorite. One day a student who played in the last row of the second violin section asked if she could submit a design. Frankly, I was a bit skeptical, because she didn't seem like a self-starter and didn't contribute too much (ok, she didn't contribute anything) musically, but I agreed, and soon she submitted a design. I was shocked! It was creative, colorful, captured the spirit of the school and the orchestra and was simply well-done! When the orchestra voted on multiple submissions, her logo won.

1 Corinthians 2:11 speaks to this idea.

"But one and the same Spirit is active in all these, distributing to each person as He wills."

God has gifted each of us in a particular manner, and sometimes a person might not be operating in their area of primary giftedness. Whether we serve in management, ministry, or any leadership capacity, we should seek to discover the giftedness of each person for whom we are responsible and put *that* gift to use. We would be amazed at the hidden talents residing beneath the surface of our colleagues.

13-BOY OR BEAN BAG?

I have been watching with interest the dialogue concerning biological males competing in female athletic events. When I was a kid, we would choose sides to play softball at recess and the girls were always selected last. Why? Because they were designed differently, and the boys thought that the girls would be a liability. While that wasn't always the case, you could be confident that the team captain would select the guys first, and the girls last.

Now it seems that when a biological male identifies as a female and wants to compete in a female sport, "he" believes that he has an advantage…and he does. "He" is designed differently than his female counterparts, giving him a decided advantage.

I can identify as a cardboard box, but I doubt that Fed-Ex would ship me to Chicago. Why? Because I fail to meet the requirements necessary to act as a cardboard box. I can identify as a bean bag…the constitution gives me that right, but I doubt that you would play corn hole with me. I don't meet the requirements necessary to actually be used as a bean bag. I am designed differently.

When a person makes a decision, they must live with the consequences of that choice. It seems that in today's culture, a person can adopt an aberrative lifestyle, then require everyone *else* to accommodate them by using new pronouns to identify them and then create laws that deem that lifestyle to be not only acceptable but normal. In other words, everyone except the person who identifies in a certain way has to pay the consequences of that person's life choice. This is just not right.

Biological males should compete with biological males, and biological females should compete with biological females. Biological males should use restrooms and locker rooms designed for biological males. If you desire to identify as a female, that puts YOU in a bind when it comes to athletics and restrooms, not the rest of the country. Accept the consequences of your decisions rather than expecting the other 95% of Americans to adapt to your life choices as normal.

Now if you will excuse me, I am going to head down to Fed-Ex to see if they will ship me to Bakersfield.

14-A CHANGED LIFE

John was a rebellious young man. His mother died when he was seven years old, and he was raised by a strict, distanced father. By the age of eleven he was working for his father. After joining the Navy, his defiant attitude earned him both punishment and a demotion. Knowing only sea life, he went to work on board a ship that carried slaves out of South Africa, eventually becoming a captain.

It was on one of those voyages that a terrible storm threatened to sink the ship. Remembering his mother's Godly influence, and a book she had read to him as a child entitled "The Imitation Of Christ", John called out to God to spare his life and save his soul. Miraculously, some cargo shifted, plugging a hole in the side of the ship, and it drifted to safety.

John decided to go all in, and began to prepare for the ministry, ultimately becoming pastor in Olney, Buckinghamshire, England. It was there that he penned a song that is estimated to be sung some ten million times a year and has been recorded over 11,000 times. In 1967 it was recorded by singer Joan Collins and stayed on the charts for 67 weeks. His song? John Newton's "Amazing Grace":

Amazing grace
How sweet the sound
That saved a wretch like me.
I once was lost, but now I'm found
Was blind, but now I see.

'Twas grace that taught my heart to fear
And grace my fears relieved;
How precious did that grace appear
The hour I first believed.

The Lord has promised good to me,
His word my hope secures;

He will my shield and portion be
As long as life endures.

15-COVERED

I was sitting on our apartment porch early one morning, when a disheveled young man appeared from between the two storage units across the street. I immediately noticed something missing: his pants! He slowly made his way over to the fence separating the apartment complex from the street, looked at me pleadingly and asked, "Sir, do you have any pants I could borrow?" I wasn't about to *loan* him any pants, but I looked through my dresser and found a pair of shorts that I could part with and tossed them over the fence to him. "Thank you, Sir! It has been a rough night!" I replied, "I can only imagine!"

That episode got me to thinking. How had I reacted when confronted by someone who had been exposed in front of me? Perhaps an ungodly lifestyle had been exposed, or an idiosyncrasy that caused embarrassment. Maybe a habit had been laid bare, or an attitude that was counterproductive. Had I quickly shared with someone, "Have you heard about....?" Did I discuss this "exposure" behind their back? Or did I assist them in "covering up?"

Psalm 32:1 says, *"Blessed is the one whose transgressions are forgiven, whose sins are covered."*

Psalm 85:2 puts it this way, *"You forgave the iniquity of your people and covered all their sins."*

I was convicted that day to do all that I could to cover the exposure of those who were embarrassed, rather than add to their embarrassment by exploiting what I knew to their chagrin. We all have "blind spots" that need to be corrected, and a true friend lovingly corrects, then protects. Remember the golden rule. How would you like to be treated when something that causes embarrassment is exposed? "Do unto others…"

16-IN THE FIRE

As I watched the flames licking at the firewood in the fireplace this morning, I was reminded of three guys who were thrown into the fire and not only survived but thrived. Their names were Hananiah, Mishael and Azariah, but the chief official of the Babylonian empire had their names changed to Shadrack, Meshack and Abednego. (My dad called them "Yourshack", "Myshack" and "Abungalow", but that is a story for another time.)

These guys refused to bow down to the ninety-foot-tall golden idol of the king and were thrown into a furnace that was so hot that it killed the men who were charged with depositing the three men of Israel into the furnace. Then the king saw something that froze him in his tracks. "Didn't we throw three men, bound, into the fire??...Look, I see four men, not tied, walking around in the fire unharmed; and the fourth looks like a son of the gods!!!" (Daniel 3:24-25)

Have you ever been in the fire? When I was fired from a church because I changed the pastor's wife's seat in choir, I was in the fire...*But Jesus was with me*!! When my son split his head open in a bicycle accident and things looked grim for a while, *Jesus was with me*! I don't know your specific circumstance, but I am confident that when you went through the fire, *Jesus was with you!*

Isaiah 43 records a beautiful promise to Israel, but it applies to today's believers as well:

> *Now this is what the Lord says-*
>
> *The One who created you, Jacob-*
>
> *The One who formed you, Israel-*
>
> *"Do not fear, for I have redeemed you;*
>
> *I have called you by your name; You are Mine.*
>
> *I will be with you when you pass through the waters...*
>
> *You will not be scorched when you walk through the fire,*
>
> *And the flame will not burn you." (vs. 1-2)*

When you walk through the inevitable fire, take heart! God walks with you, holds you by the hand and says, *"Do not fear, I will help you."* (Isa. 41:13)

My junior year at Wheaton Academy I decided to go out for the wrestling team. My dad wasn't too happy because I was there on a trumpet scholarship and he envisioned my lip in twelve pieces, but I was determined. We practiced at the Wheaton College wrestling practice facility, where they kept the temperature at a cool 102 degrees, promoting weight loss. We ran up and down several stories of steps, worked on moves and sweated...a lot!

One day I had given my very best. We had trained especially hard that day, and then paired off with partners in our weight class to practice moves. I worked and worked and couldn't seem to grasp the particular move we were being taught. Finally, I collapsed with my back to the wall, sobbing uncontrollably.

"What's the matter, Gage?" The coach asked.

"I just can't do it! I have tried and tried and I just don't get how to make that takedown!"

The coach sat down by me and put his arm around my shoulder. "It's ok, man. You will get it. It takes time. Just keep trying."

And I did. And that year I won the Junior varsity championship in our league in my weight class...a whopping 120 lbs.

Philippians 3:13 and 14 gives us this instruction,

"Forgetting what is behind I press on toward the goal to win the prize for which God has called me..."

Here the Apostle Paul uses the imagery of athletic competition to encourage his readers to not give up, but keeping their eyes on the finish line, to press on...That is great advice. The race isn't always easy. There is discouragement, exhaustion, fierce competition, inadequate preparation. There is opposition, distraction and conflict. But press on, NEVER GIVING UP! And when you finally cross the finish line you will hear " Well done, my good and faithful servant."

18-LUIGI

Luigi was born on a boat outside the town of La Havre, France while his parents were returning to their homeland of Italy after visiting relatives in America. Luigi's father was a wood carver, and by the age of twelve Luigi was carving animals out of wood. Realizing that he had a unique gift, he was sent to the nearest carving school in Austria, then back to Venice, Italy to study the art of carving.

In 1910 Luigi accepted a position in Barre, Vermont carving headstones. Returning to Italy in 1917 he fought for his mother country against Prussia, then returned to Vermont to continue his headstone carving. He carved more than 500 headstones during his career. In 1933 he was introduced to a sculptor by the name of

Gutzon Borglum who hired him as a stone carver specializing in granite. The two men would work together until Borglum's death in 1941.

In 1925, Borglum was asked to design a sculpture in the mountains of South Dakota commemorating selected heroes of the west: Lewis and Clark, Buffalo Bill Cody, Indian guide Sacagawea and Chief Red Cloud, but Borglum felt that US presidents representing 150 years of US history would be more appropriate, so he began work on Mt. Rushmore. Over 400 miners and craftsmen worked on the mountain, removing large chunks of granite with well-placed dynamite, but Borglum soon realized that a gifted craftsman would be required to add the necessary detail to add emotion to the project.

And so it was that Luigi Del Bianco, an Italian immigrant to America, hung suspended 500 feet above the ground with the sun beating down on his neck and the fine granite dust turning his face white as he put the finishing touches on the faces of George Washington, Thomas Jefferson, Teddy Roosevelt and Abraham Lincoln.

We are a land comprised of people from various backgrounds, nationalities, social strata and ethnic cultures. We are young, old, rich, poor, short, tall, weak and strong. But we are all Americans. Let's celebrate our diversity while joining our hearts in unity in gratitude for the visionary leaders who have led us to where we are today, the *United* States of America.

19-PEACE IN THE MIDST OF A STORM

David is King of Israel, but his son Absolom desperately wants to sit on the throne. II Samuel 15 records an attempted coup by

Absolom, who sets up a temporary throne in Hebron and sends criers all over the countryside announcing that Absolom is now the king. David, realizing that a mutiny is in process, takes his family and 600 faithful followers and escapes from Jerusalem to the northeast, where they hide out. Even some of David's most faithful counselors appear to have sided with Absolom, and the situation looks desperate for David.

It is at this point in the story that David writes Psalm 3.

"But You, Lord, are a shield around me…"(v.3)

"I lie down and sleep; I wake again because the Lord sustains me.." (v. 5)

"Salvation belongs to the Lord!" (v.8)

Have you ever been overwhelmed with resistance? Does it seem as if the whole world is against you? STAND FAST! Our salvation comes from the Lord, who, even in the most desperate circumstances allows us to lie down and sleep peacefully, confident that HE will win the battle!

In the ensuing battle David's forces win and Absolom is killed. While David grieves the death of his son, his kingdom is spared and his life is protected. Sometimes the battle causes casualties, but in the end, God protects and provides. "Even when I go through the darkest valley, I fear no danger, for You are with me…" (Psalm 23:4) Someone once wisely said, "The situation is desperate but WE are not desperate." Trust Him to carry you through the darkest night. He is sufficient.

Exodus 1 shares an interesting story of two courageous women; Shiprah and Puah. The Pharoah who had invited Joseph's family to live in Egypt has died, and another Pharoah has taken his place. Not familiar with the history between Joseph's family and the previous Egyptian monarch, the new Pharoah sees the nation of Israel exploding numerically. Fearing a mutiny, he commands the midwives of the Israeli people to allow baby girls to live but kill all baby boys. Shiprah and Puah disobey and refuse to terminate the pregnancies of the baby boys. After a while, Pharoah calls them in.

"Why have you not done what I told you to do? There are more baby boys around here than there ever were!!"

"Well, the Israeli moms are too strong and healthy…the babies are born before we can even get there!"

As a result of the defiance and stand of these two midwives, baby Moses is born. And God rewards both midwives by giving them fruitful families. Rabbinical literature claims that these two and their families escaped Egypt with the Israelis during the exodus.

God rewards courage. He rewards taking a stand against evil and doing the right thing. In what ways are you being called to be courageous? Take a stand. Be brave. Do the right thing. God will reward your faithfulness and obedience. It is very possible that you and generations to follow will be blessed by the stand you take today.

21-A BOY BORN DEAD

On October 28, 1953, a little baby boy was born dead in Jonesboro, Arkansas. The doctor laid the lifeless body aside while attending to the birth mother, but eighteen minutes later they heard a gasp and the little baby had miraculously resuscitated! Deprived of oxygen to the brain for those initial minutes, baby David was left with cerebral palsy.

By the age of fourteen David was orphaned and was passed from home to home and family to family, finally arriving in an abusive home that left him feeling unwanted and unloved. He endured constant physical pain and ridicule from his classmates, and attempted suicide on several occasions. In 1970 his sister led him to faith in Christ, giving him a reason to live.

David Ring went on to graduate from William Jewel college and began a ministry of motivational speaking in churches and other venues. He now ministers to over 100,000 every year. David says, "God took my greatest liability and made it my greatest asset." In challenging people to share their faith without fear, his signature line is "I have cerebral palsy...what's your excuse"?

God can and will use anyone who is willing. He is not as interested in your *ability* as He is your *availability*. What assets have been given to you by God that could be used for His glory? Most of us don't deal with the challenges that David Ring* has had to face, so "what's your excuse"?

*davidring.org

22-AWESOME GOD

"Now Mount Sanai was all in smoke because the Lord descended upon it in fire; and its smoke ascended like the smoke of a furnace, and the whole mountain quaked violently." (Ex. 19:18)

Exodus 19 instills both fear and awe in the heart of the reader. In this chapter we catch a glimpse of the other-worldly holiness of God. We see His power, His glory, His majesty and splendor to the point that mankind cannot even look upon His Presence without facing immediate death.

In verses 10 and 11 God tells Moses to have the people prepare for three days for His visit. In verse 12 and 13 God establishes the boundaries for interacting with His presence, warning of immediate death for anyone who violates those boundaries. In verse 20 God descends upon the mountain and speaks with Moses, and immediately warns again of the judgement that will follow if the boundaries are breached, and again in verse 24 God warns the people to pay attention to the boundaries He has established in order for the people to come near His presence.

For years I have focused on the love of God: his compassion, His tender mercies and His longsuffering patience, and I still believe in each one of those attributes. But we must never forget His Holiness, His Almighty Power, and the awesome other-worldliness of His presence. He isn't "The Man Upstairs", He isn't "The Big

Guy," He is far beyond our wildest comprehension. He is incomprehensible.

Even though "God is love" (1 John 4:7) we should approach Him reverently, cautiously, optimistically and with a great sense of awe and wonder. We can't explain Him, we can simply rest in the knowledge that if we come through Jesus, He accepts us and makes us part of His great family. We can only approach God on His terms and with the utmost sense of respect, humility and reverence. We can say with Moses,

"Lord, who is like You among the gods? Who is like You, glorious in holiness, revered with praises, performing wonders?" (Ex. 15:11

23-AN OLD NEW THING

I did something last night that I never thought I would do again...I played trumpet in an orchestra rehearsal at our church! Here is the back story:

In 2019 I was diagnosed with neuropathy, and all of my muscles quit working, including my facial muscles. After 65 years of playing trumpet, I quit playing and didn't touch a horn for three years. A couple of months ago a lady in choir asked my wife Ruthie if I would consider teaching their 9- year- old son trumpet ...so I pondered that and decided I would try to get back in shape to the point that I could at least demonstrate to a 9 -year- old! I bought a cheap horn through a friend, and another friend got me a couple of trumpet method books, and I practiced twice a day, thirty minutes each time. After a month I thought I could at least demonstrate simple concepts, so I started teaching him. But I wasn't satisfied with only playing enough to teach, so I increased my practice and then I wondered if I could get back in shape to the point that I could play a third trumpet part in church orchestra...so I requested the music and began to practice that. And last night was the culmination of a lot of hard work and determination!

Here is the point: God may have a place of service waiting for you...but He might be waiting for YOU to prepare! When Paul was mentoring the young preacher boy Timothy, he advised him to

"Study and be eager to do your utmost to present yourself to God approved (tested by trial)." (2 Tim. 2:15, Amplified Bible)

The wisest man who ever lived put it this way,

"Whatever your hands find to do, do with all your strength..." (Ecclesiastes. 9:10)

To give your best requires effort, time and sacrifice, but the results are more than worth the investment. Howard Grose was serving as minister of music in the late 1800's when a young man came in very late to choir practice. When Grose questioned the young man as to the reason for his tardiness, the man simply shrugged his shoulders. Grose responded, "The Lord doesn't want your spare time!" Motivated by this event, Grose went on to pen the words to this hymn:

"Give of your best to the Master;

Give of the strength of your youth;

Throw your soul's fresh, growing ardor

Into the battle for truth.

Jesus has set the example,

Dauntless was he, young and brave;

Give Him your loyal devotion;

Give him the best that you have."

24-CARRYING SOMEONE ELSE'S BURDEN

I was officially diagnosed with neuropathy in 2019 but had symptoms for some ten years before that. As the condition worsened, my neurologist recommended a treatment plan that required 15 applications at $125-$200 each. For months we negotiated with our insurance company to cover the treatments, but they considered them "experimental" and refused to cover the cost. Then one day we received a check from a dear friend that was neither expected nor requested. That check completely covered the cost of the treatments, and at least for a while, I saw improvement in my condition.

Galatians 6:2 speaks to this act of generosity:

"Carry one another's burdens; in this way you will fulfill the law of Christ."

Just exactly what is the "law of Christ"? Luke 10:27 gives us a hint:

*"You shall love the Lord your God with all your heart, with all your soul, with all your strength, and with all your mind, **and your neighbor as yourself.**"*

This statement was taken from a passage known as the SHEMA, which means "listen", or "hear", and it is quoted daily to this day by our faithful Hebrew friends. It comes from Deuteronomy 6:5, which says,

"Hear, O Israel: The Lord our God, the Lord is one. Love the Lord your God with all your heart and with all your soul and with all your strength."

But Jesus added "and your neighbor as yourself" to illustrate that loving God naturally leads to loving others and sharing their heavy loads!

Bearing the burdens of another is an act of encouragement, an act of faithfulness, and an act of compassion. But it is also a testimony! Imagine the impact of lending a helping hand to an unsaved neighbor or friend! What a tremendous affirmation that being a believer goes beyond simply talking about your faith but puts feet to your testimony!

How can you *"carry one another's burden"* today? When you find a way and act on it, you are being obedient to the very words of Jesus.

In Exodus 4, God calls Moses to lead the Children of Israel out of bondage. Moses says, "But I stutter!" So Yahweh replies, "I will send Aaron your brother to help you."

Fast forward to the confrontation through which Pharoah was finally convinced to let the people go.

Ex. 7:10- When Pharoah asks for a miracle, AARON throws down his staff and it becomes a serpent.

Ex. 7:19 (Nile turns to blood)- "So the Lord said to Moses, TELL AARON to stretch the staff over the waters..."

Ex. 8:5 (frogs)- "Then the Lord said to Moses, TELL AARON, 'stretch out your staff..'"

Ex. 8:16 (gnats), "Then the Lord said to Moses, 'TELL AARON...'"

Ex. 8:24 (flies) "And the LORD did this..."

Ex. 9:6 (the death of all livestock), "The LORD did this the next day.."

Ex. 9:10 (boils), "MOSES threw the soot toward heaven and it became boils…"

Ex. 9:23 (hail), "So MOSES stretched out his hand.."

Ex. 10:13 (locusts), :So MOSES stretched out his hand.."

Ex. 11:22 (darkness), "So MOSES stretched out his hand….."

Ex. 12:29, (The death of the firstborn) "Now at midnight THE LORD struck every firstborn male in the land of Egypt….

Here is the lesson: The first three plagues were initiated by Aaron. The next two the Lord took care of personally…and the next four Moses initiated. WHY? Because Moses had to learn that God can use ANY willing vessel. It doesn't matter whether one has a speech impediment, is lame, is blind, has cerebral palsy…God is willing to use ANY vessel who is willing to be used. Once Moses learned that God turned him into one of the greatest leaders the world has ever known.

Don't look at your liability or your inability. Our availability leads to God unleashing HIS ability. He can do mighty wonders through any willing vessel.

Exodus 2 recounts an event in Moses' life that would change the course of history. Moses witnesses an Egyptian overlord being incredibly cruel to an Israeli worker, so Moses kills the Egyptian and buries him. The next day he realizes that his deed is public knowledge, so he flees to an area in the desert known as Midian and takes a job herding sheep for a rancher named Jethro. Eventually Moses falls in love with the rancher's daughter Zipporah, marries her and they have two sons.

After God calls Moses to lead the children of Israel to safety, Moses decides that the safest place for Zipporah and their two boys would be back at the ranch in Midian, so he sends them back. Then, after Moses successfully leads the Israelites to safety, Jethro, Zipporah and the two sons come to visit Moses. Jethro watches Moses spend the entire day solving disputes, giving spiritual advice and making decisions. At the end of the day Moses is exhausted and Jethro gives him some wise, fatherly advice.

"What you're doing is not good...the task is too heavy for you. You do what God called you to do...instruct them in God's laws and teach them how to live and behave. But select capable men, God-fearing, trustworthy and honest. Place them over smaller groups of the people and let them settle the disputes, bringing only the most

egregious cases to you. Then you will be able to endure...
(Exodus 18:17-23)

Moses heeds the wise advice of his father-in-law, and suddenly his task becomes much more manageable. He can now accomplish the assignments for which he is singularly responsible, and others can handle the lesser responsibilities. This is timely advice for those in leadership positions, especially for those in ministry. One person can't do everything, nor should they be expected to. Delegating certain responsibilities to others frees leadership to accomplish the primary tasks to which God has called them and helps one avoid burnout. Tasks can be performed with excellence because now there is time to weigh the best solutions and make the most beneficial decisions.

When asking a well-known pastor about his time management practices, he replied, "You can't manage time; you can only manage yourself." And the best way to manage yourself is to find capable people to whom you can delegate appropriate responsibilities. Then you can all accomplish much more than you ever could by yourself.

27-REMEMBERING GOD'S PROVISION

"In days to come, when your son asks you, 'What does this mean?'
say to him, 'With a mighty hand the Lord brought us out of Egypt,
out of the land of slavery." (Ex. 13:14)

In Exodus 13 Moses commands the Israelites to commemorate their freedom through a series of observations, including eating unleavened bread and sacrificing first-born animals. Later in their journey, as God wins battles on their behalf, they will erect rock monuments called "ebenezers" (meaning "stone of help") as reminders of God's faithfulness to them. But this observation is different. After 400 years of bondage which had grown increasingly burdensome, they are finally free. In Exodus 13:14 Moses tells us why this celebration was to be different. It is to be a reminder to future generations of God's faithfulness and power. In the previous chapter God reiterates the importance of this celebration, "Celebrate this day as a lasting ordinance for the generations to come." And to this day that commemoration is observed by our Hebrew friends. It is known as Passover.

Our children and grandchildren need to know how and when God has intervened in our lives. It is important to celebrate God's protection and provision. For years I wondered about the date of my spiritual birthday. Fortunately, my mom kept a diary and added important details every day of her life. One day I called her and asked her to look back in her diaries to discover the day I gave my life to Christ. She quickly called back.

"July 30, 1955."

And that day has been important to me ever since, as my spiritual birthday.

What days are important to your family as days when God supernaturally intervened on your behalf? Celebrate those days. Remember God's goodness. Remember His faithfulness. Then when you face difficulty and trials you can lean on what God has done in the past to give you confidence for the future. Just as the Israelites did.

"Then Aaron and Hur supported his hands, one on one side and one on the other so that his hands remained steady until the sun went down. So Joshua defeated Amalek and his army with the sword." (Exodus 17:12-13 HCSB)

Esau and Jacob (who would be re-named Israel) were twin brothers and had been at odds with each other since Jacob deceived their father into giving *him* the birthright which should have been Esau's by right. Now, hundreds of years later, we see the tribe of Amalek, the grandson of Esau, going to war against the children of Israel. Moses instructs Joshua to go to battle with the Amalekites, and he goes to the top of a nearby hill. As long as Moses has his hands lifted over the battlefield, Joshua and his forces prevail, but as soon as Moses drops his arms, the Amalekites began to take the upper hand. Moses' brother Aaron and Miriam's husband Hur come to the rescue by supporting the arms of Moses through the battle, and Joshua's army defeats the forces of the Amalekites.

The story is told of a farmer who belonged to the local church but never attended. One winter day the pastor visited the farmer. As they sat by the fireplace the pastor asked why he never saw the farmer in church.

"I can be just as religious sitting on my porch as I can sitting in the pew." The farmer declared.

The pastor stood up, grabbed the fireplace tongs, removed a coal from the fireplace, placed it on the hearth and sat down. They continued chatting for a time, and then it was time for the pastor to leave.

"Well look at that!" The pastor exclaimed! "That coal on the hearth has completely gone out!"

Sure enough, the coal was sitting alone and cold on the hearth.

"You may feel fulfilled sitting on your porch on Sunday, but the fact is, we need you and you need us to keep the fire burning in our hearts."

We have an enemy who wants us to be cold, devoid of passion and indifferent. But when we hear the testimonies of others in whom God is working, when we hear a challenging message from God's Word, when we worship as a family and fellowship together it gives us courage. It gives us boldness. It keeps the fire and passion burning in our hearts. It is each of us holding up the arms of the others, encouraging each other to persevere and to finish well.

We need each other. Let's hold each other's arms up so that we can win the battle!!

29-THE FIRST SONG

The first two songs recorded in the Bible are both found in Exodus 15. The first is known as "Moses' Song" and gives us a healthy template for worship today. This song includes:

What God has done:

"In the greatness of Your majesty You threw down those who opposed You." (v.7)

What God is doing:

"The Lord is my strength and defense; He has become my salvation." (v.2)

What God will do:

"In Your unfailing love You will lead the people You have redeemed." (v.13)

Then Moses' sister Miriam picks up the refrain and praises the Lord for the great victory He has won:

"Sing to the Lord

For He is highly exalted.

Both horse and driver

He has hurled into the sea."

Worship should reflect this outline:

What God has done,

What God is doing,

What God will do.

Both Miriam and Moses could face the future with confidence because God had been faithful to rescue them in the past. In the same way, we can be confident of the future as we look back at the victories God has already won.

30-THE MOUSE

Recently we had a dead mouse under our deck...it smelled...bad! We couldn't disassemble the deck to retrieve him because of the way the deck boards were attached to each other, and we couldn't reach him by going under the foundation boards. An anti-odor spray could be applied through the cracks, but that was a temporary fix at best. We just had to wait until the poor guy...disappeared ...to relieve the repugnant odor.

This experience caused me to reflect on our culture. Bad people do bad things because they are...dead! We can't expect dead people to act like ones who are alive. What we *can* do is love them to Jesus and occasionally spray the perfume of patience, tolerance, diplomacy and a sweet spirit around them until they gain...life.

In discussing the faith of Abraham, the apostle Paul refers to the God of Abraham as the God:

"who gives life to the dead and calls into being things that were not." (Romans 4:17)

When I was on a mission trip to El Salvador, I was asked to preach for an outdoor service. Not being a great speaker, I used the only thing I could think of as an illustration. I held up my trumpet and said, "Blow, trumpet, BLOW!!" Of course, it remained silent. Then I explained that for that instrument to play a tune, someone had to breathe life into it.

God is the only one who can breathe life into a dead thing and cause it to emit a pleasant odor. Since dead things naturally smell bad, do all that you can to introduce the life-giver to those friends, family and acquaintances who desperately need to come alive. When we impact our culture for Christ, we will begin to notice the stench of death being replaced by the sweet aroma of the presence of the Holy Spirit in our midst.

31-TO SERVE AND PROTECT

Recently my devotional reading led me to Psalm 25…here are the last couple of verses:

"Guard my soul and deliver me;

Do not let me be ashamed,

for I take refuge in Thee.

Let integrity and uprightness preserve me,

For I wait for Thee.

Redeem Israel, O God,

Out of all his troubles." (Psalm 25:20-22 NASB)

On October 7, 2023 Addir was attending a music festival on farmland near the Israel-Gaza border. Born and raised in New York, the 23- year-old was with several childhood friends. As they were resting in tents at the conclusion of the festival, they heard sirens, then rockets exploding close to them. They hurried toward their car and sought safety in a small bomb shelter. Addir heard Arabic and machine gun fire and suddenly knew that they were under attack by terrorists. As they peeked out of the shelter to see what was happening, they saw terrorists throwing grenades into nearby shelters. Instructing the girls who were with them to hide, Addir and his friends burst out of the shelter and rushed the terrorists in an effort to distract them. They were immediately gunned down, but 6 hours later the girls were rescued by Israeli forces. Addir and his two friends were buried side by side, with 3,000 attending their funeral.

When we think of the word "safety" we often need to also consider the word "sacrifice." Often our safety comes at the expense of someone willing to sacrifice on our behalf. Psalm 36:7 makes this observation:

"How precious is Your lovingkindness, O God! Therefore the children of men put their trust under the shadow of Your wings."

But the safety that we enjoy under the shadow of the Father's wings came at a very high price. Someone had to suffer and die to purchase our freedom. In fact, it cost the Father everything to make a way to guarantee our safety. Because of this great sacrifice we can say with the Psalmist, "Guard my soul and deliver me…for I take refuge in Thee."

32-TOMORROW

The Nile has turned to blood, but Pharoah isn't convinced to let the Israelites go. So Moses and Aaron initiate a plague of frogs. In Exodus 8:8 Pharoah begs Moses and Aaron to get rid of the frogs, so Moses replies, "I will leave it up to you to decide when the frogs disappear." And Pharoah inexplicably says, "TOMORROW!"

"I like frogs in my bed, And frogs in the tub,

frogs in the soup and frogs in the mud.

Frogs in the baby's crib, Frogs on the wall,

Frogs in the shower and Frogs at the mall!"

Pharoah could have said, "NOW! Get rid of the frogs NOW!" But he didn't say that. He said, "Just give me one more night with the frogs."

How often do we try to get rid of a bad habit, a dysfunctional relationship, a hurtful practice, only to say, "I will deal with this tomorrow. Just give me one more night with the frogs."

When you are convicted about a harmful practice, a bad habit, an omission of something you should be doing…deal with it now. Don't wait until the problem gets bigger and more difficult to handle. Do it now. Then you won't have to spend one more night with the frogs

33-NOW I BELIEVE!

"When Israel saw the great power that the Lord used against the Egyptians, the people feared the Lord and believed in Him and in His servant Moses." (Exodus 14:31)

It appears that the Israelites crossed the Red Sea at night, because during the morning watch, which would have been 2 AM to 6 AM, God threw the Egyptian army into confusion as they chased Israel onto the dry ocean floor, causing their chariots to crash into each other and the chariot wheels to become loose. Psalm 77:16-20 recounts this event and refers to a terrible storm on the Egyptian side of the cloud, with heavy rain, thunder, lightning, even an earthquake, but the Israeli side of the cloud experienced clear and dry passage through the walls of water that had been gathered up on both sides.

At daybreak God commands Moses to stretch out his hand over the walled water, causing the receding ocean to come crashing down on the Egyptian army. Exodus 14:28 solemnly reports, "None of them survived." The Israelites saw the lifeless bodies of the defeated Egyptian army, and "the people feared the Lord and believed in Him and in His servant Moses." (Ex. 14:31) This is quite a contrast to the attitude they displayed just 20 verses prior to this event, when they accused Moses of leading them out of Egypt only to have them "die in the wilderness." What changed their perspective?

Faith is "the substance of things hoped for, the evidence of things not seen." (Hebrews 11:1) Even though Israel had observed the ten plagues that eventually led to their release, they still didn't have faith to believe that God could rescue them…they only saw their immediate circumstances. But God rescued them anyway, and after they had seen the Divine intervention that led to their freedom, they believed. Rather than focusing on their lack of faith, notice that when they saw God act, they believed.

Recognizing God's intervention in our lives increases our level of faith. Remembering victories He has won in the past gives confidence for the future, reminding us that if He has rescued us before, He can do it again. Recognize His supernatural activity in your life and face the future with confidence. If He has rescued you before, He can rescue you again!

34-ENOUGH IS ENOUGH!

It took the death of Pharoah's firstborn to finally persuade him to release the Israelites from Egyptian bondage.

"GO and worship the Lord as you have requested…take your stuff and GO!"

"And also bless me."

WHAT??

After hardening his heart nine times, and then losing his son and seeing many other grieving parents as their firstborn sons die during the night, Pharoah finally releases Moses and the Israelites, but then he adds one final surprising request: "*And also bless me.*" Had Pharoah finally come to the realization that the God of the Israelites was the one true God? Had he had a spiritual renewal? If so, his revival was short-lived, because soon after this event he rallies his troops, changes his mind about his offer to let Israel go and chases them down, hoping to bring them back to Egypt.

But for a moment…for a brief instant...Pharoah saw Jehovah for who He was…All-powerful, victorious, capable of accomplishing His purpose in the face of any opposition, and he asked Moses to pray for him. He was asking that these plagues disappear, never again to bring calamity to the Egyptian people. He was saying enough is enough!

Often God uses difficulty, trials and tragedy to draw the hard-hearted to Himself. We need to be sensitive to these opportunities to encourage and to "bless" those for whom we have been praying. Often difficult circumstances can open a door for ministry. Be aware and ready to encourage and support in tragic situations. When someone says, "enough is enough", the time may be right for ministry and encouragement.

"Do not be conformed to this age, but be transformed by the renewing of your mind, so that you may discern what is the good, pleasing, and perfect will of God." (Romans 12:2)

William Paterson Nicholson was saved out of a very sinful lifestyle through the prayers of a faithful, godly mother, and went on to prepare for the ministry at the Bible Training Institute of Glasgow, Scotland. His preaching was uniquely touched by God, and countless lives were changed through his ministry. After years of effective preaching around the world he returned to Ireland. Intending to stay a few weeks, his tenure there turned into six years of wonderful ministry with thousands coming to know Christ. In the province of Ulster revival broke out with one church reporting over 2,000 professions of faith and another reporting 1,500 conversions. At the famed Harland and Wolff shipyard a special building had to be built to house the stolen tools that were returned by workmen who had accepted Christ. (Evangelical-times.org, accessed 3.8.23 at 11:30 AM)

When Christ impacts a life, change is inevitable. Zacchaeus is a great example. After he met Jesus, he gave half of his wealth to the poor and paid back four times to those he had defrauded. (Luke 19:8) Nicodemus went from a skeptical Pharisee to one who anointed the body of Jesus with a very expensive mixture of myrrh and aloes (Luke 19:39). The Samaritan woman at the well changed from a life of promiscuity to a missionary who brought many to Jesus (John 4).

Galatians 5 lists the behavior of those who don't know Jesus, then lists the changes that result from a relationship with Christ: love, joy, peace, patience, kindness, goodness, faith, gentleness and self-control. We can evaluate the genuineness of our walk with Jesus based on the fruit produced in our lives. If we can't see a change from our previous way of life, we should question the validity of our commitment to Jesus.

In Matthew 7 Jesus says, "You will recognize them by their fruit." What fruit do people observe in you?

36-VISION

Jim was born in 1875 to a Missouri minister-farmer. Not being able to afford college, he worked on his father's farm for two years after high school, then learned the dry goods business from a family friend. In 1897, on the advice of his doctor, he moved to the drier climate of Colorado. There he met Tom Callahan and Guy Johnson, and Jim became a sales clerk at their dry goods and clothing store, The Golden Rule. Impressed by his work ethic, they offered him a management position at their Evanston, Wyoming store.

In 1902, Johnson, Callahan and Jim became one-third partners in a new Golden Rule store in Kennemer, Wyoming. By 1907, Jim bought out the interests of the other two investors in the store and began to expand with stores in Utah and Idaho. By 1917 there were 175 stores. And Jim….James….James Cash Penney was on his way to transforming the retail business by "selling good quality merchandise at reasonable prices, offering good customer service, and sharing profits with associates…" (https://txarchives.org/smu/finding_aids/00012.xml)

The key to J.C. Penney's success was *vision*. He was always looking ahead, seeing not just what was, but what could be. In a letter to an unknown recipient on American Airlines stationery, J.C. Penney once wrote, "Sorry to say that my eyesight is impaired, but thank God that my vision is not!"

Proverbs 29:18 says, "Where there is no vision the people are unrestrained, but happy is he who keeps the law." (NASB) The word "vision" here means the "prophetic Word of God…" or being guided by Biblical principles. Conversely, the ones who know and keep God's law are happy, or successful, or blessed. They are looking at what is ahead, not what is behind. They have vision.

J.C. Penney was guided by Biblical principles instilled in him by his pastor-father. The result of his vision, driven by applying Biblical values was a peak number of 2,053 stores by 1973. Know God's Word and apply it to whatever you are doing. Always "press on" toward what is ahead, "forgetting what is behind." (Phil. 3:13-14) Vision will allow you to see the big picture. It will give direction. It will lead to blessing and success in accomplishing your goals. And it will keep you moving forward.

37-THE PLAN

The late Bob McKenzie, former president of Benson Publishing Company, quoted Bill Gaither as saying, "Have a plan and work your plan. If you aren't working your plan, you are working someone else's plan." I have reflected on that statement many times. In ministry, what is my plan? I understand that collaboration with a pastor and other team members or staff members is a necessity, but what is MY plan? Do I just float between the ideas of those around me, or am I headed in a definite, pre-conceived direction?

The Bible has a lot to say about the importance of having a plan:

"Plans fail for lack of counsel, but with many advisers they succeed." (Prov. 15:22)

"Commit to the Lord whatever you do, and he will establish your plans." (Prov. 16:3)

"Many are the plans in a person's heart, but it is the Lord's purpose that prevails." (Prov. 19:21)

"Plans are established by seeking advice; so if you wage war, obtain guidance." (Prov. 20:18)

"The plans of the diligent lead to profit as surely as haste leads to poverty." (Prov. 21:5)

What can we learn from these verses? Here are a few principles:

1) Seek God FIRST.
2) When creating a plan, seek Godly counsel from others.

3) Make your plan flexible so God can change your course if necessary.
4) Include others in formulating your plan.
5) Don't make your plan hastily. Think about it, pray about it, view it from every possible angle before implementing it.

Yogi Berra once wisely said, "If you don't know where you are going, you'll end up someplace else." Have a plan and work your plan so you will end up where you want to be.

38-WHAT A CIRCUS

I have had some interesting experiences playing in the band for the circus. There was the time the parade of elephants blew snot all over the band on their way by…then the time that a contractor hired us to play the circus, but the musicians from the local union all showed up to the rehearsal in tuxes with their instruments expecting to play even though they hadn't been hired! Then there was the time that I punched a hole through my lip after playing 3 shows on Saturday and had to hire a sub to take my place for the Sunday shows.

But the greatest learning experience came from the first circus I ever played. The circus band has a two-hour rehearsal on Tuesday afternoon, but the opening Tuesday night show is three hours long. That means that the band sight reads one hour of the first show, having never seen the music before. How in the world can a musician play an hour of the first show without rehearsing the material? *By practicing sight-reading for years before that technique is ever needed.* Part of my practice regimen has always been to find a new excerpt or exercise and play through it, noting problem areas; rhythms, intervals, chromatics, etc. that might be challenging, then going back over the difficult spots until they can be played smoothly. By preparing to sight-read, one can accomplish much when called upon to use that technique under the pressure of performance.

The apostle Paul addresses this issue in 2 Timothy 2:15,

"Work hard so you can present yourself to God and receive His approval. Be a good worker, one who does not need to be ashamed..." I tell my trumpet students, "Don't practice until you get it right. Practice until you can't get it wrong." That applies to our spiritual preparation as well. We should know God's Word to the point that when called upon, we can bring to mind verses of encouragement, salvation, caution, confidence and hope. We should spend enough time with the Father that we know His heart and can trust Him even in the most difficult circumstances. Don't wait until you need to know before you learn. That is too late. Prepare now for what you will need later. You will be glad you did!

39-WINDFALL

I had been praying for a windfall but received something far more valuable. We had home repairs that were desperately needed. We would have liked to take a trip, but it cost too much. It would have been nice to be able to have had the trees pruned, but that was expensive. But here is what happened!

As I was praying, we received an unexpected rebate from the hospital for an overpayment of a copay in the amount of $180. Within two days, the "check engine" light in the car came on, so we took it in for a much-needed oil change. The engine light was still on, so we went to Auto Zone and had them run a diagnostic test, which showed that the car needed a radiator flush and new coolant. The oil change and radiator flush cost a total of $170. And here is the lesson:

"My God will supply all your needs according to His riches in glory in Christ Jesus." (Phil. 4:19)

"What man among you, if his son asks him for bread, will give him a stone? Or if he asks for a fish, will give him a snake? If you then, who are evil, know how to give good gifts to your children, how much more will your Father in heaven give good things to those who ask Him!" (Matthew 7:9-11)

God doesn't always give us what we *want*, and we don't always receive what we *think* we need, but God always provides what we need it, when it is needed. And He is usually one step ahead of us, providing what we must have before we need it. Trust him. Completely. And thank Him in advance for His provision.

"Count your blessings, name them one by one;

Count your blessings , see what God hath done;

Count your blessings, name them one by one;

And it will surprise you what the Lord hath done." (Johnson Oatman)

Bezalel and Oholiab may not be household names, but these two guys were crucial to the spiritual lives of Israel because their craftsmanship was characterized by excellence. Their skill was so legendary that God specifically requested that they be in charge of overseeing and building the tabernacle which would represent the presence of God among the people. Exodus 36:1 states,

"Bezalel, Oholiab, and all the skilled people are to work based on everything the Lord has commanded. The Lord has given them wisdom and understanding to know how to do all the work of constructing the sanctuary."

Bezalel and Oholiab were instructed to construct the tabernacle based on the design the Lord had given, and verse 2 of Exodus 36 follows up with,

"So Moses summoned Bezalel, Oholiab, and every skilled person in whose heart the Lord had placed wisdom, everyone whose heart moved him, to come to the work and do it. "

Why did God select these two, one from the tribe of Judah and one from Dan to complete the construction of the tabernacle? Because they didn't take shortcuts, they didn't undermine the integrity of their work with shoddy, cost-cutting effort that barely got by. They gave 100% effort 100% of the time, and that attention to detail and the reputation they had earned placed them among the top two builders in Israel!

Legendary musician/pastor Derric Johnson defines excellence this way, "the point where passion meets precision." It takes both an emotional investment and a high level of craftsmanship to accomplish work with excellence.

Martin Luther once said, "A Christian shoemaker doesn't do his duty by putting little crosses on his shoes. He does his duty by making *really good shoes!*"

The name Bezalel means "resting in God's shadow". When our work is characterized by excellence, we can rest in the assurance that the Heavenly Father is pleased with our effort and our work is a reflection of *His* character.

41-YOU CAN FIX IT!

My two-year-old granddaughter has been visiting this week, and she has been pure joy! She is talking up a storm and loves to play with my toy trucks. Yesterday she had a toy semi-truck, and the cab became disconnected from the trailer. She held it up to me and said, "You can fix it, Grandpa!" What blind faith! No hesitation but complete confidence in Grandpa's ability to fix what was broken.

Have you ever messed up and felt like you were irreparably broken? No failure is beyond repair, given a penitent heart and God's ability to restore. Jeremiah 33:6 puts it this way,

*"**Nevertheless**, I will bring health and healing to it; I will heal my people and let them enjoy abundant **peace and security**."*

Here are two observations:

1) The word "nevertheless." No matter what causes the failure, no matter how egregious the failure may be, the Father can fix it.

2) "Peace and security". When we face failure, discouragement or disappointment, our peace and security are in jeopardy. But when the Father fixes our brokenness, peace and security follow.

Give your broken pieces to the Father and pray, "Here Father. You can fix it!" And He will.

42-THE SWEETNESS OF THE WORD

*"The ordinances of the Lord are reliable
and altogether righteous.*

*They are more desirable than gold—
than an abundance of pure gold;
and sweeter than honey,
which comes from the honeycomb.*

*In addition, Your servant is warned by them;
there is great reward in keeping them." (Psalm 19:9-11)*

Psalm 19 is a microcosm of Psalm 119, where all 176 verses discuss the benefits of God's law, precepts, Word...His communication with us. In Psalm 19 David refers to the benefits of God's Word and compares God's communication with us to the sweetness of honey.

When Hebrew children were learning to read and write, the teacher would write several words from the Torah (the first five books of the Old Testament) on a slate, and then drizzle the slate with honey. Then the children would be encouraged to lick the honey from the slate, demonstrating that God's Word was to be enjoyed for its sweetness.

Psalm 19 concludes with,

"May the words of my mouth
and the meditation of my heart
be acceptable to You,
Lord, my rock and my Redeemer."

Just as God's Word is sweet to us, our words should be sweet to the Father and to those around us. Then we will truly be a reflection of the Father's love to those in our sphere of influence.

43-THE CHRISTMAS TRUCE

The year was 1914, and French, German, British and Belgian troops were engaged in a conflict that would eventually claim 15 million lives. The events of Christmas Eve, 1914 are recorded in the diary of British machine gunner Bruce Bairnsfather.

Bairnsfather was shivering in his muddy, cold trench when he heard a noise from the German front. As he listened more closely, he could make out the faint sounds of Christmas carols being sung from the German side of the battlefield. Soon some of the British soldiers began to sing on their side of the front lines. Authors A.J. Baime and Volker Janssen of the History Channel report what happened next:

"Suddenly", Bairnsfather recalled, "We heard a confused shouting on the other side. We all stopped to listen. The shout came again." The voice was from an enemy soldier, speaking in English with a strong German accent. He was saying, "Come over here!"

"One of the British soldiers answered, "You come half-way. I come half-way." (Janssen, 2022)

What followed was surreal. Soldiers from both sides met in the middle of the field, shared cigarettes and wine, played spontaneous games of soccer and helped each other line up the dead bodies. They sang carols and conversed together. In the middle of a terrible war there was a period of peace.

Luke 2:14 records the voices of the angelic host raised in praise, "Glory to God in the highest, and on earth *peace* to those on whom his favors rest." No matter what battles you may be facing today, the Prince of Peace can offer serenity and solace in the midst of your darkest night.

44-GRATEFUL WHEN WRONGED

This was to have been a very special Christmas for our oldest daughter. We saved for months to get her a very special gift with tons of sentimental significance and mailed it through an international delivery company to guarantee arrival by Christmas. It finally arrived on December 28, only to discover that the package had been opened, the contents stolen, and the package re-wrapped and delivered...empty.

At first I was angry...then deeply saddened. What was to have been a very special gift was gone, leaving a sense of having been violated. Then I recalled an event that impacted theologian Matthew Henry. Robbed at knifepoint, he wrote in his diary the following day,

"Let me be thankful, first, because he never robbed me before; second, because although he took my purse, he did not take my life; third, because although he took all I possessed, it was not much; and fourth, because it was I who was robbed, not I who robbed."

In any situation we can find something for which to be grateful. Through this experience I learned some valuable insights:

1) It was only stuff. No lives were lost, no major trauma experienced except a sense of loss. Stuff can be replaced.

2) God owns everything. They didn't steal from me, but from Him. He will take care of it in His way and in His time.

3) It is a reminder that material possessions are transitory. I have never seen a casket hitched to a U-Haul trailer. You can't take anything with you, so we need to hold all of God's material gifts with an open hand and let Him put in or take out whatever He wishes.

This experience reminded me of a quote by a man who lost everything. Recorded in Job 1:21, The reaction of this man placed his priorities where they should have been,

"...The Lord gave and the Lord has taken away; Blessed be the name of the Lord."

45- "I HEARD THE BELLS"

On December 1, 1863, Henry Wadsworth Longfellow received a call that his son Charley had been grievously wounded in the Civil War battle of Mine Run. Longfellow and his son Ernest immediately headed to Washington, D.C. to bring Charley home while he recuperated from his injuries. Just two years prior to this event, Longfellow had been taking a nap when he was awakened by his wife's screams. Her dress had caught fire and Longfellow immediately jumped up and tried to extinguish the flames, first with a rug and then with his body, but the next day she passed away from her injuries. Longfellow himself was badly burned on his hands and face, and his injuries prevented him from attending his wife's funeral. He grew a beard to hide his facial injuries.

It was Christmas Eve, 1863 when Longfellow penned the words to a poem reflecting both his discouragement over life's challenges and the hope to be found in the real meaning of Christmas. The full meaning of this song can only be realized when each successive verse is seen as a single story:

"I heard the bells on Christmas Day
Their old, familiar carols play,
and wild and sweet
The words repeat
Of peace on earth, good-will to men!

And thought how, as the day had come,
The belfries of all Christendom
Had rolled along
The unbroken song
Of peace on earth, good-will to men!

Till ringing, singing on its way,
The world revolved from night to day,
A voice, a chime,
A chant sublime
Of peace on earth, good-will to men!

Then from each black, accursed mouth
The cannon thundered in the South,
And with the sound
The carols drowned
Of peace on earth, good-will to men!

It was as if an earthquake rent
The hearth-stones of a continent,
And made forlorn
The households born
Of peace on earth, good-will to men!

And in despair I bowed my head;
"There is no peace on earth," I said;
"For hate is strong,
And mocks the song
Of peace on earth, good-will to men!"

Then pealed the bells more loud and deep:
"God is not dead, nor doth He sleep;

The Wrong shall fail, The Right prevail,
With peace on earth, good-will to men."

46-FINAL TRANSITION

The ratio of people who have lived to people who have died is pretty amazing....it is 1:1. The Bible has a unique way of announcing the death of the Patriarchs. Here are a few examples:

Abraham- "He took his last breath and died at a ripe old age, old and contented, and he was *gathered to his people*." (Gen. 25:8)

Isaac- "He took his last breath and died, and was *gathered to his people*, old and full of days." (Gen. 35:29)

Jacob- "When Jacob had finished instructing his sons, he drew his feet into the bed and died. He was *gathered to his people*." (Gen. 49:33)

Death isn't the end. As a matter of fact, one spends a lot more time on the *other* side of death than on this side! It is a comfort to realize that when a believer passes from this life to the next, that person is *"gathered to his people"*. Those who have preceded us in physical death are waiting to welcome us to glory where we will spend eternity with our Savior and with our loved ones.

When my Grandpa Gerow (my maternal grandfather) passed away, my Grandma wrote a poem to commemorate his passing and to remind the family of the promise of eternal life:

"Home at last, the life's long journey ended!
The pilgrim's feet now tread the golden shore.
And he beholds the face of Christ His Savior,
and is at home with Him forevermore...
And so we travel on toward that glad morning
when we shall meet our loved one once again
Where there will never be another parting,
and with the Lord forever we shall reign!" (Marion Gerow)

END NOTES

The Bible answers every one of man's questions pertaining to purpose in life. The stories and anecdotes in this little book illustrate how contemporary God's Word is to answer today's challenges and to give necessary direction (and course correction) as needed. My prayer is that you will find direction and purpose, not in this book as much as in God's precious, Holy Word.